For the Love of ACT Notebook

by

The Private Prep Curriculum Team

ISBN-13: 978-0-9968322-8-1

Published by Private Prep

Printed by CreateSpace, an Amazon.com company

Contents

Introduction

Welcome to ACT prep!

As tutors with many years of experience, we know that prepping for the ACT is a process that looks different for every student. Our goal is to help you personalize the process and find what works best for you. In this book, you will find places to take notes on the most important strategies. You will also be able to take notes on which processes work best for you as you practice. We hope that this book will help you from your first day learning about the ACT to your final exam.

Happy studying! Abbey, Emily, Kyla, Mike, & Tehya

How to Use this Book

For the Love of ACT Notebook is designed to be a companion to the *For the Love of ACT* book series. The books in this series are a place to learn about each test section, including strategies and content. You will use this book alongside each chapter in the book series to take notes on what you learned. This book also contains cheat sheets for each section that you can use to review before practice tests and real tests. The Full Test Chapter is a place for you to record your progress and extend your learning.

ACT English

Time:

Number of Questions:

Number of Passages:

Questions Per Passage:

Ideal Timing Per Passage:

Chapter 2: Section Structure

Question Types...

Mechanics:

Content/Structure:

Chapter 3: Assessment

Below, list any areas of discomfort or confusion—whether from the book's assessment or your diagnostic exam.

Content Area	Question(s) from Assessment/Diagnostic	Completed?
Start this list		✓

Chapter 4: The Golden Rules

1. As I go through the section, I should read the passage...

   (A) only where there are questions
   (B) all the way through, sentence by sentence

2. As I answer a given question, I should read...

   (A) only the underlined portion that pertains to the question
   (B) the entire sentence containing the given question

3. "NO CHANGE" is the correct answer...

   (A) more often than are other answers
   (B) less often than are other answers
   (C) just as often as are other answers

4. "Shorter & Simpler = Better" pertains to...

   (A) Mechanics questions, which usually do not have an actual question
   (B) Mechanics questions, which usually do have an actual question
   (C) Content/Structure questions, which usually do not have an actual question
   (D) Content/Structure questions, which usually do have an actual question

5. Answers containing the word "being" are...

   (A) always correct
   (B) always incorrect

6. "Preceding sentence" means...

   (A) the sentence before
   (B) the sentence after

Remaining Questions

Below, list any areas of discomfort or confusion from the Practice! section of this chapter.

Question	Explanation

Chapter 5: Parts of Speech

5.1 Nouns & Pronouns

Nouns
Definition:

Examples:

Pronouns
Definition:

Examples:

5.2 Verbs

Definition:

Examples:

-ing Endings:

Examples:

5.3 Adjectives & Adverbs

Adjectives
Definition:

Examples:

Adverbs
Definition:

Examples:

5.4 Prepositions & Prepositional Phrases

Definition of preposition:

Definition of a prepositional phrase:

True or False: A prepositional phrase can contain the subject of a sentence.

Examples:

Remaining Questions

Below, list any areas of discomfort or confusion from the Practice! section of this chapter.

Question	Explanation

Chapter 6: Forming Basic & Complex Sentences

6.1 Independent & Dependent Clauses/Phrases

Independent Clauses
Definition:

Examples:

Dependent Clauses
Definition:

Examples:

Dependent Phrases
Definition:

Examples:

6.2 Putting It All Together

Write your own sentences in the following formats...

1. A sentence with a prepositional phrase:

2. A sentence with an adjective and an adverb:

3. Dependent, Independent:

4. Inde, Dependent, pendent:

5. Independent, Dependent:

Remaining Questions

Below, list any areas of discomfort or confusion from the Practice! section of this chapter.

Question	Explanation

Chapter 7: Independent vs. Dependent

How to identify the independent vs. Dependent question:

Remaining Questions

Below, list any areas of discomfort or confusion from the Practice! section of this chapter.

Question	Explanation

Chapter 8: Punctuation

Equivalent Punctuation

Directions: Fill in the blanks with the equivalent punctuation mark(s)

    1.   ; = _____

    2.   : = _____

    3.   _____ , _____ , _____ . = _____ _____ _____ . = _____ _____ _____ .

The Rules

Directions: Fill in the rule of each punctuation mark. Then, write three of your own example sentences that correctly use the given punctuation.

Semicolons

    _____ ; _____ .

    1.   _____ .

    2.   _____ .

    3.   _____ .

Semicolons are used in a list when _____ .

    1.   _____

         _____ .

    2.   _____

         _____ .

    3.   _____ .

         _____ .

Colons

    _____ : word/list/dependent/sentence/Sentence .

    1.   _____ .

    2.   _____ .

    3.   _____ .

Commas   The Rules - *continued*

The basic job of a comma is to separate _____ and _____ .

Introductory Phrase Commas: _____ , _____ .

   1. _____ .

   2. _____ .

   3. _____ .

FANBOYS Commas: _____ , FANBOYS _____ .

   1. _____ .

   2. _____ .

   3. _____ .

Adjective, Adjective Noun Commas: To test whether or not you need a comma in between two adjectives preceding a noun...

   a) _____ .

   b) _____ .

Examples

   1. _____ .

   2. _____ .

   3. _____ .

Parenthetical Commas: To test whether or not a parenthetical is correct, _____

_____

Examples...

   1. _____ .

   2. _____ .

   3. _____ .

Commas Before Quotation Marks: Commas come before quotation marks when _____

_____ , not when _____ .

Examples...

   1. _____ .

   2. _____ .

   3. _____ .

Apostrophes

For apostrophe questions, ask...

1. _____ ?
2. _____ ?

Singular	Singular Posessive	Plural	Singular Posessive
dog			
author			
parent			
friend			
teacher			
person			
man			
woman			
boss			
James			
child			

Remaining Questions

Below, list any areas of discomfort or confusion from the Practice! section of this chapter.

Question	Explanation

Chapter 9: Verbs

Whenever a verb is underlined...

1. Check _____ .

    a) Decide if "_____" or "_____" works best with each answer choice. If _____

    _____ , chose that answer.

    b) If that doesn't work, locate the subject by crossing out _____ , _____ ,

    and _____ .

    c) If you've found the subject and the answers are still unclear, replace the noun with

    _____ for a plural non and _____ for a singular noun.

2. Check _____ and _____ .

    a) Look at _____ .

Write your own...

Subject-Verb Agreement Question(s):

Tense and/or Parallelism Question:

Remaining Questions

Below, list any areas of discomfort or confusion from the Practice! section of this chapter.

Question	Explanation

Chapter 10: Pronouns

10.1 Basic Pronouns

How to identify a basic pronoun question:

How to answer a basic pronoun question:

Write your own basic pronoun question(s):

10.2 Ambiguous Pronouns

How to identify an ambiguous pronoun question:

How to answer an ambiguous pronoun question:

Write your own ambiguous pronoun question(s):

10.3 Who vs. Whom

Who is a _____ , while *whom* is a _____ .

- Try replacing *who* with _____ .
- Try replacing *whom* with _____ .
- If the "who vs. whom" is in a prepositional phrase, only _____ is acceptable.

Remaining Questions

Below, list any areas of discomfort or confusion from the Practice! section of this chapter.

Question	Explanation

Chapter 11: Modifiers

11.1 Basic Misplaced & Dangling Modifiers

How to identify a misplaced/dangling modifier question:

How to answer a misplaced/dangling modifier question:

Write your own misplaced/dangling modifier question(s):

11.2 Comparison Modifiers

How to identify a comparison modifier question:

How to answer a comparison modifier question:

Write your own comparison modifier question(s):

Remaining Questions

Below, list any areas of discomfort or confusion from the Practice! section of this chapter.

Question	Explanation

Chapter 12: Parallelism

Parallelism is...

Common parallelism structures:

Remaining Questions

Below, list any areas of discomfort or confusion from the Practice! section of this chapter.

Question	Explanation

Chapter 13: Diction & Idioms

Diction & Idiom questions look like...

Tips & Tricks:

Below, record unfamiliar instances of diction/idioms with their definitions as you find them.

Diction/Idiom	Definition

Remaining Questions

Below, list any areas of discomfort or confusion from the Practice! section of this chapter.

Question	Explanation

Chapter 14: Which Best

How to answer a "which best" question:

Remaining Questions

Below, list any areas of discomfort or confusion from the Practice! section of this chapter.

Question	Explanation

Chapter 15: Transition Words

How to identify and answer transition word question:

How to answer a transition word question:

How to answer a transition word question:

- If deleting or omitting the transition word is an option, that answer is usually _____ .

  Just make sure to check that _____ .

Below, record unfamiliar transition words with their definitions as you find them.

Transition Word	Definition

Remaining Questions

Below, list any areas of discomfort or confusion from the Practice! section of this chapter.

Question	Explanation

Chapter 16: Placement

To answer a placement question, pay close attention to...

1. _____

    Examples:

2. _____

    Examples:

3. _____

    Examples:

Remaining Questions

Below, list any areas of discomfort or confusion from the Practice! section of this chapter.

Question	Explanation

Chapter 17: Adding, Deleting, & Revising

Do not add or get rid of information when...

Add or keep information when...

How to use the second half of add/delete/revise answers:

Remaining Questions

Below, list any areas of discomfort or confusion from the Practice! section of this chapter.

Question	Explanation

Chapter 18: Writer's Goal

To answer a writer's goal question...

Remaining Questions

Below, list any areas of discomfort or confusion from the Practice! section of this chapter.

Question	Explanation

Chapter 19-22: The Essay

Essay Topic:

Brainstorm:

Outline

Introduction
    General sentence introducing the topic:_____

_____

_____

    Thesis Statement:_____

_____

    Road Map:_____
Body Paragraph # 1
    Topic_____

    Supporting Evidence_____

_____

_____

_____

Body Paragraph # 2
    Topic_____

    Supporting Evidence_____

_____

_____

_____

Body Paragraph # 3
    Topic_____

    Supporting Evidence_____

_____

_____

_____

Conclusion
    Restate Thesis:_____

_____

_____

*Star where you address a counterargument

Notes for Improvement

Essay Topic:

Brainstorm:

Outline

Introduction
    General sentence introducing the topic:_____
_____
_____

    Thesis Statement:_____
_____

    Road Map:_____
Body Paragraph # 1
    Topic_____
    Supporting Evidence_____
_____
_____
_____

Body Paragraph # 2
    Topic_____
    Supporting Evidence_____
_____
_____
_____

Body Paragraph # 3
    Topic_____
    Supporting Evidence_____
_____
_____
_____

Conclusion
    Restate Thesis:_____
_____
_____

*Star where you address a counterargument

Notes for Improvement

Essay Topic:

Brainstorm:

Outline

Introduction
    General sentence introducing the topic:_____
_____
_____

    Thesis Statement:_____
_____

    Road Map:_____
Body Paragraph # 1
    Topic_____
    Supporting Evidence_____
_____
_____
_____

Body Paragraph # 2
    Topic_____
    Supporting Evidence_____
_____
_____
_____

Body Paragraph # 3
    Topic_____
    Supporting Evidence_____
_____
_____
_____

Conclusion
    Restate Thesis:_____
_____
_____

*Star where you address a counterargument

Notes for Improvement

Essay Topic:

Brainstorm:

Outline

Introduction
    General sentence introducing the topic:_____

_____

_____

    Thesis Statement:_____

_____

    Road Map:_____

Body Paragraph # 1
    Topic_____

    Supporting Evidence_____

_____

_____

_____

Body Paragraph # 2
    Topic_____

    Supporting Evidence_____

_____

_____

_____

Body Paragraph # 3
    Topic_____

    Supporting Evidence_____

_____

_____

_____

Conclusion
    Restate Thesis:_____

_____

_____

*Star where you address a counterargument

Notes for Improvement

Chapter 22: Practice Test 1

Use the table below to record unfamiliar, confusing, or incorrect questions from this practice test, along with notes to help you better understand how to correctly answer similar questions moving forward.

Question #	Question Type	Notes

Chapter 23: Practice Test 2

Use the table below to record unfamiliar, confusing, or incorrect questions from this practice test, along with notes to help you better understand how to correctly answer similar questions moving forward.

Question #	Question Type	Notes

ACT English Cheat Sheet

The Golden Rules

Answer every question.   Read the passage all the way through, sentence by sentence.

"being" = wrong   Read the whole sentence before answering the question.

"preceding" = before   No question, just answers? Shorter & Simpler = Better

Mechanics

. = ; = , ForAndNorButOrYetSo   Inde, dependent, pendent.

Independent: word/list/dependent/sentence/Sentence.   Inde (dependent) pendent.

adjective, adjective noun = adjective and adjective noun ✓   Inde—dependent—pendent.

Only use this comma, "when this is an actual quote."   Dependent, independent. // Independent, dependent.

Semicolons separate items; in a list when at least one item; in the list; has, at least, one comma; in it.

's - singular possessive, s' = plural possessive EXCEPT pronouns and already plural words (ex: children, women, etc.)

they're = they are	it's = it is	children's = belonging to children
their = belonging to them	its = belonging to it	**childrens = not a word**
there = a place	**its' = not a word**	**childrens' = not a word**

Underlined verb:

1. Check Subject-Verb Agreement

   a. Match answers with "it" or "they." If one answer is the odd one out, pick that answer.

   b. OR cross out prepositional phrases, parentheticals, or any dependents to find the subject.

   c. If you've found the subject and still can't tell which answers agree, swap in "they" for a plural noun or "it" for a singular one.

2. Check tense and parallelism by looking at nearby, NONunderlined verbs.

Pronouns:

- Basic: match the pronoun to the word it's replacing and make sure the two agree.

- Ambiguous: three answers with generic pronouns and one (correct) answer that's a specific noun

- Who vs. Whom → subject vs. object → replace with "he" vs. replace with "him"

Looks like they're changing **word order**? Check modifiers.

- "Running down the hall, my book fell" means "my book was running down the hall and fell." ✗

- *The word directly after the comma in a "dependent, independent" is doing the dependent.*

- "Running down the hall, I dropped my book" means "I was running down the hall and dropped my book." ✓

many = countable → many days (1 day, 2 days, 3 days, etc. ✓)   -er = comparing 2 things

much = uncountable → much sand (1 sand, 2 sands...no ✗)   -est = comparing 3+ things

Parallelism: keep things in the same structure/form if you see...

- a list (dancing, baking, and ~~to hike~~ hiking)   - "either...or..."

- "not only...but also..."   - "neither...nor..."

- "if...then..."   comparisons with "than" or "as"

ACT English Cheat Sheet - continued

Content & Structure

Which Best → underline + follow the directions → detailed, vivid, specific = good

Transition Words

1. Read the preceding sentence. What was it about?

2. Read the sentence with the underlined transition word WITHOUT the transition word. What was it about?

3. How do those two ideas relate? Contrast? Causation? An example?

4. If deleting/omitting the transition word is an option, that is the **correct** answer (unless you're making an "independent, independent.")

Placement: sequence of events, transition words, words that signify familiarity (ex: that day)

Add/Delete/Revise: scope, topic, redundancy

Writer's Goal: reread title and topic sentences

ACT Math

Time:

Number of Questions:

PART 0: assessment
TOPICS TO DISCUSS

Below, list any areas of discomfort or confusion—whether from the book's assessment, diagnostic exam, practice test or assigned homework. Be sure to include the question and test numbers.

CONTENT AREA	QUESTION(S) #	COMPLETED?

PART 1: common MISCONCEPTIONS

Below, list the **5** common misconceptions of the ACT Math Section.

1 _____

2 _____

3 _____

4 _____

5 _____

notes, NOTES, notes

_____

_____

_____

_____

_____

_____

_____

_____

_____

_____

_____

PART 2: general STRATEGIES

Below, paraphrase the 7 steps.

1 _____

2 _____

3 _____

4 _____

5 _____

6 _____

7 _____

notes, NOTES, notes

_____

_____

_____

_____

_____

_____

_____

_____

_____

PART 3: pathways AND PRACTICE

Complete the notes below. Then, use the pathways to answer the practice questions.

WORK FORWARD

Best suited for questions you can _____ the problem.

WORK BACKWARDS

Ideal for questions that ask you to solve for a single variable (like "x"), working backwards can save you time by
_____.

BE FLEXIBLE

When you get stuck on a question, it's okay to _____ directions of solving problems.

let's PRACTICE

1. Which of the following is a solution to the equation $x^2 - 100x = 0$?

   A. 200

   B. 100

   C. 50

   D. 10

   E. -10

2. When $x = 5$, which of the following is equivalent to $\dfrac{x^2 - x - 6}{x - 3}$?

   F. -2

   G. 0

   H. 4

   J. 7

   K. 15

3. Craig's Carpets is installing new carpet in a customer's living room. The installer notes that the area of a rectangular room is 120 square meters, and the perimeter is 46 meters. The installer lost the paperwork with the room's dimensions. What are the dimensions of the room, in meters?

   A. 6 by 20

   B. 20 by 13

   C. 12 by 10

   D. 15 by 8

   E. 16 by 7

4. Square ABED has a side length of 12. Point C is the midpoint of AB. What is the length of CE?

   F. 9

   G. 12

   H. $6\sqrt{5}$

   J. $\sqrt{258}$

   K. 18

PART 3: pathways AND PRACTICE

let's CHECK and REFLECT

1. **B**

WHICH PATHWAY?

Which pathway did you use to solve the problem? Why did you gravitate towards this direction?

_____
_____
_____
_____

TRY A DIFFERENT WAY, HOW DID IT GO?

Now, let's change things up! Try a new pathway for the same problem. After completing the question two different pathways, was one way more beneficial than another? Why?

_____
_____
_____
_____

2. **J**

WHICH PATHWAY?

Which pathway did you use to solve the problem? Why did you gravitate towards this direction?

_____
_____
_____
_____

TRY A DIFFERENT WAY, HOW DID IT GO?

Now, let's change things up! Try a new pathway for the same problem. After completing the question two different pathways, was one way more beneficial than another? Why?

_____
_____
_____
_____

3. D

WHICH PATHWAY?

Which pathway did you use to solve the problem? Why did you gravitate towards this direction?

_____

_____

_____

_____

TRY A DIFFERENT WAY, HOW DID IT GO?

Now, let's change things up! Try a new pathway for the same problem. After completing the question two different pathways, was one way more beneficial than another? Why?

_____

_____

_____

_____

4. H

WHICH PATHWAY?

Which pathway did you use to solve the problem? Why did you gravitate towards this direction?

_____

_____

_____

_____

TRY A DIFFERENT WAY, HOW DID IT GO?

Now, let's change things up! Try a new pathway for the same problem. After completing the question two different pathways, was one way more beneficial than another? Why?

_____

_____

_____

_____

PART 4: timing STRATEGIES

List the timing strategies below. Additional space is given for you to summarize how to use each strategy. A log is provided after the notes section to track the progress of each timing strategy and help find the optimal approach for you.

1 _____

notes, NOTES, notes

_____
_____
_____
_____

2 _____

notes, NOTES, notes

_____
_____
_____
_____

3 _____

notes, NOTES, notes

_____
_____
_____
_____

PART4: timing STRATEGIES

4 _____

notes, NOTES, notes

_____

_____

_____

_____

timing LOG

STRATEGY	BENCHMARK/START#	TIMED?(Y/N)	NOTES/SCORE

PART4: timing STRATEGIES

timing LOG

STRATEGY	BENCHMARK/START#	TIMED?(Y/N)	NOTES/SCORE

PART 5: answer choice STRATEGIES

Fill in the following notes. Under each answer choice type, list the key differences.

- Identify their _____

1. NUMBERS:

- _____
- _____

2. SPECIAL VALUES:

- _____
- _____
- _____
- _____

3. EXPRESSIONS:

- _____
- _____
- _____
- _____
- _____
- _____

4. PHRASES:

- _____
- _____
- _____

PART 5: *answer choice* STRATEGIES

5. VISUALS:

- _____
- _____
- _____
- _____
- _____

notes, NOTES, notes

_____
_____
_____
_____
_____
_____
_____
_____
_____
_____
_____
_____
_____
_____
_____
_____
_____
_____
_____
_____
_____
_____
_____
_____
_____
_____

PART 6: *question type*
STRATEGIES

3. VISUALS BASED QUESTIONS:

step 1 _____

step 2 _____

step 3 _____

step 4 _____

step 5 _____

step 6 _____

notes, NOTES, notes

_____

_____

_____

_____

4. CLUSTER QUESTIONS:

step 1 _____

step 2 _____

step 3 _____

step 4 _____

step 5 _____

notes, NOTES, notes

_____

_____

_____

_____

PART 6: question type STRATEGIES

Paraphrase or summarize the steps below.

1. WORD PROBLEMS:

step 1 _____

step 2 _____

step 3 _____

step 4 _____

step 5 _____

notes, NOTES, notes

_____

_____

_____

_____

2. EXPRESSION BASED QUESTIONS:

step 1 _____

step 2 _____

step 3 _____

step 4 _____

step 5 _____

step 6 _____

notes, NOTES, notes

_____

_____

_____

_____

CHEAT SHEET: math

CHECKLIST

☐ Calculator Charged?/ Batteries packed?

☐ Degree Mode Set?

general

1. Focus on question statement
2. Determine answer format
3. Setup solution (should you work backwards? forwards?)
4. Check back in with the answers often, and eliminate choices as you go
5. Simplify last; keep checking in and eliminating answer choices
6. Re-read question to make sure you solved the problem
7. Choose your final answer

PATHWAYS

- It's okay to work forwards or backwards.
  - If you get stuck, change directions!
- When working backwards, its ok to invent a number for x
  - Rule of thumb: avoid using 0,1, or 2
- If answers are numerical, plug in!
- When in doubt, draw it out!
  - Particularly useful for word problems!!

timing

- Remember the test starts easy and ends hard
- Trust your journey: what strategy worked best?
  - Watch the clock and set a goal
    - 30 questions in 30 or less (adjust based on accommodation)
  - Working the section backwards
    - Starting on the hardest questions will speed you up
  - Reducing the test
    - What is your benchmark goal?

CHEAT SHEET: math

QUESTION TYPES

- Expression
  - Avoid going on solving for x autopilot
    - ■ Re-read the ? statement; ask yourself if you answered it
- Word Problem
  - Avoid reading!!!
  - Focus on the question statement
- Visual Based
  - Remember the figures are drawn to scale for the most part
  - Avoid reading text: the label on the figure can often lead you to what you are solving for

answer choice

- Numerical
  - Good for working backwards; plug them in!
  - Simplify completely, if working forwards
- Special Value
  - Avoid simplifying your answer to a number
- Phrases
  - Focus on what's false or true, and eliminate accordingly!
- Expressions
  - Set-up these problems; you don't have to solve for a value!
  - To work backwards, inventing a value for x (eg. 3) works best!
- Visuals
  - Focus on what you know about the type of graph
    - ■ Roots, x-intercepts, y-intercepts, specific coordinates, etc.

ACT Reading

Time:

Number of Questions:

Number of Passages:

Questions Per Passage:

Chapter 1: The Basics

There are 4 genres (passage types) that always appear in the same order.

Genre in Order of Appearance	Definition	Example Topic

Every Reading section will have a paired passage in which two shorter passages (Passage A and Passage B) have questions both about each individual passage and that compare and contrast the two together.

_____ *True or False: The paired passage can show up on any genre.*

Chapter 2: Reading Comprehension

Annotation

Annotating is the act of underlining and circling as you read.

What are the 5 key details to look for as you read and annotate?

C _____

L _____

O _____

S _____

E _____

Annotation - *continued*

Notice that these create a convenient acronym: CLOSE. Remember, we want to always be using CLOSE reading on the ACT.

Which of these details tends to be the most important? _____

Some people find it helpful to create an annotation key and stick to it, using a different symbol for each of the five key details. Create your annotation key below.

Annotation Key
C
L
O
S
E

Textual Mapping

In a textual map, you write one word (or a short phrase) in the margins that summarizes the main idea of each paragraph. This creates a visual guide (a map!).

Theme

_____ + _____ = Theme

Examples

		Theme

How do you find the theme?

1. The most important paragraph is usually the _____ because it summarizes the author's final claim.

2. Also, the _____ paragraph is really helpful because it introduces the topic.

3. The key components of the author's argument are found in the _____ sentences.

4. Of the 5 CLOSE details of your annotations, _____ is especially helpful for understanding the theme.

Tone

Tone is how the author feels about a specific subject. It's a distinct emotion.

How do you find the tone?

1. Look at the _____, where authors often "set the tone."

2. Look at the _____, where authors often reinforce their argument.

3. Of the 5 CLOSE details of your annotations, _____ is especially helpful for understanding the tone.

Use the following table to keep track of vocabulary related to tone words.

Negative	Neutral	Positive

Critical Reading of Questions and Answer Choices

It's not just the passages that you need to use your reading comprehension skills for. The ACT is really good at writing answer choices that are almost right. Since it's a Multiple Choice test, it's important to remember that this is an "all or nothing" test–one wrong word makes the whole answer choice wrong. **Almost correct is incorrect.**

Pay close attention to the most common traps the ACT sets:

1. Be mindful of action words (verbs). Examples include words like the following:

   a. _____

   b. _____

   c. _____

Critical Reading of Questions and Answer Choices - *continued*

2. Be mindful of specific language (nouns). Examples include words like the following:

    a. _____

    b. _____

    c. _____

3. Be mindful of extremes. Examples include words like the following:

    a. _____

    b. _____

    c. _____

Chapter Test

Below, list any areas of discomfort or confusion from the Chapter Test.

Question	Explanation

Chapter 3: Question Categories

There are three main ACT Reading Question categories:

1. _____

2. _____

3. _____

Specific Detail Questions

These questions test one key skill: close reading. All you have to do is FIND the detail, and then closely read the sentences around it. Precision is key!

There are 4 steps to answer these questions:

1. _____

2. _____

3. _____

4. Read through the answer choices. Pick the answer that matches your own.

How can you more quickly find answers?

Look for **locator words**. Examples include things like:

- _____

- _____

- _____

To find locator words more quickly, scan the text from _____ .

- Trust your visual map (or your textual map if you created one!). Thinking about where on the page you saw a certain phrase helps you know where you need to return.

- If you can't remember where to find the information and the locators aren't helping, the best part of each paragraph to read will be the _____ .

_____ *True or False: Specific Detail questions are the most common questions in the ACT Reading section.*

_____ *True or False: The ACT asks you to think critically and analyze the text, rather than taking the language at a surface level.*

_____ *True or False: On the ACT's Reading section, "inference" is just another word for "paraphrase."*

Main Idea Questions

These questions ask you to summarize paragraphs or full passages.

_____ + _____ = Main Idea

When finding the Main Idea of the whole passage, there are key places to look in order to verify your anticipated answer based on your initial read through:

1. First, read the _____ .

2. Next, read the _____ .

3. Then, consider the _____ .

Purpose Questions

These questions don't ask what the passage is saying. They ask you _____ it's being said.

Key words indicate Purpose questions. Examples include things like:

- _____

- _____

- _____

In order to answer these questions, you need to think like the author!

1. _____ the lines in question.

2. _____ would someone write this?

Because perspective is so important on these questions, let's review some key vocabulary. Fill in the definition for each term below:

First-person point of view	
Third-person point of view	
Limited point of view	
Omniscient point of view	

Chapter Test

Below, list any areas of discomfort or confusion from the Chapter Test.

Question	Explanation

Chapter 4: The Toolbox

More than any other section on the ACT, maximizing the allotted time that you have on Reading comes down to learning how to play the game of the test. The personalized plan that you develop will be built based on what allows you to maintain the highest accuracy and the fastest speed.

The following questions allow you to explore various strategies to maximize your speed.

Reordering the Passages

The ACT will always present all four passages in the same order. However, that doesn't mean you have to do them in the order they appear!

1. Is there one particular passage type that you're always able to complete the fastest? _____

_____

2. Is there one particular passage type that requires you to work more slowly? _____

_____

3. Is there one particular passage type that you really like? _____

_____

4. Is there one particular passage type that you really don't like? _____

_____

Reordering the Passages - *continued*

Some students prefer to do their fastest/favorite passages first. That lets them use all remaining time for their slowest/least favorite passages without feeling rushed.

Some students prefer to do their fastest/favorite passages last. They know that even in a time crunch, they can still see the accuracy they are capable of on these passage types.

Which student are you?

  A) Save the Best for Last

  B) Save the Worst for Last

If you don't have a preference one way or the other but you still want to explore reordering passages, you may find it helpful to **Save the Paired Passage for Last**, regardless of which genre it is. That way, even if you're pressed for time, you can still get through one of the shorter passages in full (plus, the questions are organized for you!).

The Read

Reading less of each passage can be a valuable time-saving strategy.

1. Right now, are you reading every passage all the way through? _____

   _____

2. Right now, are you skimming every passage instead of reading every word? If so, do you have

   an organized plan to skim? _____

3. Are there some passages that you think you might be able to read less of in order to save time?

   If so, which ones? _____

There are three popular ways to read the passages. Fill in the information below describing each method:

	Ideal Reading Time Per Passage	Works Well with...	Method
Read-It-All			
Outline Method			
⅔ Method			

Even if you don't think reading less will be an option for you, you won't know until you try. It can be a powerful option, even if it is only used on a single passage. Reading less buys you more time to answer the questions.

Timing

Being mindful of the clock is sometimes enough in and of itself to stay on pace, aiming to hit a particular time for all four passages. Other students prefer to spend more time on one specific genre as they know they can make up time on others.

For students with regular time, here are the most common timing breakdowns. If you have timing accommodations, or if you want to explore other timing breakdowns, your tutor will help you fill out the blank chart.

	Tried It?	Liked It?	How did you split your time on each genre?
9, 9, 9, 8 minutes			
11, 8, 8, 8 minutes			
10, 10, 10, 5 minutes			
11, 11, 11, 2 minutes			

	Tried It?	Liked It?	How did you split your time on each genre?
minutes			
minutes			
minutes			
minutes			

Reordering Questions

As it stands, ACT Reading questions aren't organized in order of difficulty or sequence, so doing them in the order they appear isn't very efficient.

1. Right now, are you answering the questions in the order they appear? _____

_____

2. If you are skipping around, do you have an organized plan to do so? _____

_____

Reordering Questions - *continued*

Answering the questions that are easiest to find first allows you to return to the text multiple times before you have to look for answers that are harder to find. This cuts down on dead time spent skimming and also allows you to build a stronger understanding of the passage's organization and main ideas.

Questions can be organized into Tiers:

	Definition	Example
Tier 1		
Tier 2		
Tier 3		

Guessing Strategies

• If two answer choices are more _____ to each other than to others, the correct answer is likely one of these two!

• The _____ answer is almost always correct. The test avoids _____.

Examples include things like:

• _____

• _____

• _____

Chapter Test

Below, list any areas of discomfort or confusion from the Chapter Test.

Question	Explanation

Chapter 5: Practice Test 1

Use the table below to plan your strategy for Practice Test 1. This will allow you to keep track of which strategies are effective and which still need to be revised.

Planned Passage Order	Planned Time Strategy	Planned Reading Method	# Correct / Score	Notes
Example: Save paired passage for last	10-10-10-5	Outline method for NS, Read-it-all for the other passages	24/40	Used an extra minute on SS so ran low on NS

Use the table below to record unfamiliar, confusing, or incorrect questions from this practice test, along with notes to help you better understand how to correctly answer similar questions moving forward.

Question #	Question Type	Notes

Chapter 6: Practice Test 2

Use the table below to plan your strategy for Practice Test 2. This will allow you to keep track of which strategies are effective and which still need to be revised.

Planned Passage Order	Planned Time Strategy	Planned Reading Method	# Correct / Score	Notes
Example: Save paired passage for last	10-10-10-5	Outline method for NS, Read-it-all for the other passages	24/40	Used an extra minute on SS so ran low on NS

Use the table below to record unfamiliar, confusing, or incorrect questions from this practice test, along with notes to help you better understand how to correctly answer similar questions moving forward.

Question #	Question Type	Notes

Chapter 7: Practice Test 3

Use the table below to plan your strategy for Practice Test 3. This will allow you to keep track of which strategies are effective and which still need to be revised.

Planned Passage Order	Planned Time Strategy	Planned Reading Method	# Correct / Score	Notes
Example: Save paired passage for last	10-10-10-5	Outline method for NS, Read-it-all for the other passages	24/40	Used an extra minute on SS so ran low on NS

Use the table below to record unfamiliar, confusing, or incorrect questions from this practice test, along with notes to help you better understand how to correctly answer similar questions moving forward.

Question #	Question Type	Notes

ACT Reading Cheat Sheet

Structure
4 passages, 10 questions per passage (40 questions in total)
35 minutes (with regular time)
Passage Genre Order:
1. Prose Fiction/Literary Narrative
2. Social Science
3. Humanities
4. Natural Science
1 paired passage that can show up on any genre

Reading Comprehension

Chronology
Lists/Repetition
Opposition/Contrast
Specialized Language
Emotional Language/Opinion
Textual Mapping: write one word/phrase to
summarize each paragraph

Topic + Argument = Theme
Tone: how an author feels about the subject
(positive, negative, or neutral)
Read the questions just as closely as the passage.
Almost correct is incorrect! Avoid extremes!

Question Categories
1. Specific Detail
2. Main Idea
3. Purpose (Why is this word/phrase/paragraph here?)

1st-person = I/we/our; 3rd-person = he/she/they
Limited = one person's viewpoint; Omniscient = "all knowing"

The Tool Box

Reordering the Passages:
- Save the best for last
- Save the worst for last
- Save the paired passage for last

Timing:
- 9-9-9-8
- 10-10-10-5
- 11-11-11-2
- Something else!

The Read:
- Read-it-All
- ⅔ Method
- Outline Method

Reordering Questions:
- Tier 1: clear locators (specific line numbers or paragraphs)
- Tier 2: everything else!
- Tier 3: ALL CAPITAL LETTERS, chronological sequence, Main Idea

---

ACT Science

Time:

Number of Questions:

Number of Passages:

Questions Per Passage:

Chapter 1: The Basics

When utilizing locators, I should ask myself:

1. _____am I looking?

2. _____am I looking for?

When completing math without a calculator on the science section, the number 629 should instead be thought of as _____.

When extrapolating a trend from a graph, I should _____ the line with my pencil.

Data bridging involves linking two or more tables or figures together. What clue might a question start with to signal a data bridge is involved?

Chapter 1: The Basis Test Timing Sheet

Record your time spent for each passage here:

Passage	Time
I	
II	
III	
IV	
V	
VI	

Remaining Questions

Below, list any areas of discomfort or confusion from the Chapter Test.

Question	Explanation

Chapter 2: Advanced Questions Types

When using the *full sentence answer choices* tactic, try to find exact _____ in the words and phrases of answer choices.

1. A chemist hypothesized, after reading the procedure of Experiment 1, that more milligrams of copper chloride would yield a larger absorbance of light at 450 nm. Do the data support her claim?

   A. Yes, because according to Table 1, as the mass of copper chloride increased the A_{450} increased.
   B. No, because according to Table 1, as the mass of copper chloride increased the A_{450} increased.
   C. Yes, because according to Table 1, as the mass of copper chloride decreased the A_{450} increased.
   D. No, because according to Table 1, as the mass of copper chloride decreased the A_{450} increased.

Does identifying differences in answer choices help with *where* to look OR *what* to look for?

Once you've identified the two data points of a mixing question, do you typically use the sum or average of those two points?

The answer to an inference question is typically _____ in the passage, but rather in the_____.

Chapter 2: Advanced Questions Test Timing Sheet

Record your time spent for *each* passage here:

Passage	Time
I	
II	
III	
IV	
V	
VI	

Remaining Questions

Below, list any areas of discomfort or confusion from the Chapter Test.

Question	Explanation

Chapter 3: Scientific Method

In a table, the independent variable is typically located in the _____-most column, whereas the dependent variable is typically located in the _____-most column.

In the table below, circle Independent or Dependent as the table header for each column.

Table 1	
Independent or Dependent	Independent or Dependent
0.05	0.09
0.10	0.21
0.15	0.30

On a figure, the independent variable is typically located in the _____-axis, whereas the dependent variable is typically located in the _____-axis.

On the figure below, circle either independent or dependent for the x and y axes.

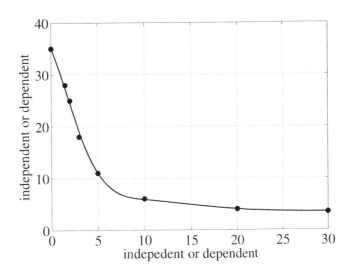

Constants of an experiment are typically _____ on a figure or table.

If a figure has generic labeling, the differences between trials are probably located somewhere in the _____ or in a _____.

What is a control group?

Create Your Own Experiment

In the table below, write down the elements of your own experiment.

Element	Description
Independent Variable 1	
Independent Variable 2	
Independent Variable 3	
Dependent Variable	
Control Group	

Chapter 4: Beating the Last Question

What makes an inverse trend trickier than a direct trend?

Below, draw an example plot of an inverse trend.

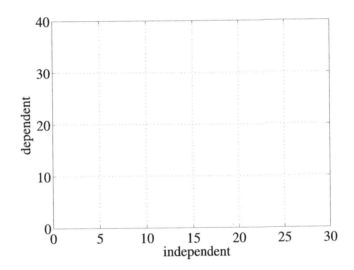

Potential energy is energy at_____, while kinetic energy is energy in_____.

In a physics circuit, current, I, and resistance, R, have an_____relationship.

The freezing point of water at standard pressure is_____degrees Celsius.

The boiling point of water at standard pressure is_____degrees Celsius.

In a chemical equation, are the number of moles of a compound located in the coefficient number at the front of the compound or in the subscript number after the compound?

Chapter 3 & 4: Test Timing Sheet

Record your time spent for *each* passage here:

Passage	Time
I	
II	
III	
IV	
V	
VI	

Remaining Questions

Below, list any areas of discomfort or confusion from the Chapter Test.

Question	Explanation

Chapter 5: Attacking Conflicting Viewpoints

Sister sentences are _____ sentences from each _____ that are essentially the same sentence with one or two different _____.

How is a conflicting viewpoints passage different from a reading passage? How is it similar?

Chapter 5: Test Timing Sheet

Record your time spent for *each* passage here:

Passage	Time
I	
II	
III	
IV	
V	
VI	

Remaining Questions

Below, list any areas of discomfort or confusion from the Chapter Test.

Question	Explanation

Chapter 6: Practice Test 1

Now practice timing yourself every 3 passages. Record the time spent on passages 1-3 and the time spent on passages 4-6 in the table below.

Passage	Time
1 to 3	
4 to 6	

Use the table below to record unfamiliar, confusing, or incorrect questions from this practice test, along with notes to help you better understand how to correctly answer similar questions moving forward.

Question #	Question Type	Notes

Chapter 7: Practice Test 2

Passage	Time
1 to 3	
4 to 6	

Use the table below to record unfamiliar, confusing, or incorrect questions from this practice test, along with notes to help you better understand how to correctly answer similar questions moving forward.

Question #	Question Type	Notes

Addendum Extra Timing Sheets

Test:_____
Record your time spent for each passage here:

Passage	Time
I	
II	
III	
IV	
V	
VI	

Test:_____
Record your time spent for each passage here:

Passage	Time
I	
II	
III	
IV	
V	
VI	

Test:_____
Record your time spent for each passage here:

Passage	Time
I	
II	
III	
IV	
V	
VI	

Test:_____
Record your time spent for each passage here:

Passage	Time
I	
II	
III	
IV	
V	
VI	

Addendum Extra Timing Sheets

Test:_____
Record your time spent for each passage here:

Passage	Time
I	
II	
III	
IV	
V	
VI	

Test:_____
Record your time spent for each passage here:

Passage	Time
I	
II	
III	
IV	
V	
VI	

Test:_____
Record your time spent for each passage here:

Passage	Time
I	
II	
III	
IV	
V	
VI	

Test:_____
Record your time spent for each passage here:

Passage	Time
I	
II	
III	
IV	
V	
VI	

ACT Science Cheat Sheet

Overall Mindset

- Where am I looking?

- What am I looking for?

- Within a passage, questions start easy and then get harder. Every time you turn the page, reset your difficulty anticipation.

- Keep it simple and direct.

- If you get lost in a question, reset. You are probably looking at the wrong data or looking for the wrong term/number/unit.

For Data Passages:

- You'll see more complex data.

- You'll have to bridge the data together at times. Look for the variable that exists in both pieces of data as a way to connect them together.

- Careful of double data and altitude/depth y-axes.

For the Last Question of Each Passage:

- Inverse relationships are more popular.

- Outside knowledge? If you don't know it, move on.

- Should involve multiple steps. If you only used one step to arrive at your answer, you are probably wrong.

- If you tend to be short of time, guess quickly on these questions and keep moving towards the end of the section.

For Research Summaries:

- Use your scientific method training! Remember that independent variables typically appear in the left-most column of a table, and the x-axis of a figure. If a time variable is the x-axis, then your independent variable is probably in the key or legend. Also remember that the dependent variable is probably your right-most column in a table or y-axis on a graph.

- Bridge the experiments together.

- What are your variables? Constants?

- How do the experiments differ?

For Conflicting Viewpoints:

- Find the sister sentences, one from each perspective.

- Keep it simple: straightforward answers are the ones to look for.

- Do not treat it like a reading passage; instead, treat it like a science passage with words.

Lastly:

- Keep moving. One of the most important factors for your science score is finishing the section or getting to as many questions as you can.

- Fight the fatigue. We know it is the last section and your energy is going to be low, but try to ignore that feeling and keep pushing!

Homework Log

Use these pages to track your timing, strategies, and results on homework sections.

Section Name	Planned Time Strategy	Section Strategies	# Correct / Score	Notes
Example: Reading PT 1 - For the Love of ACT Reading	10-10-10-5	Order: save paired passage for last	24/40	Used an extra minute on SS so ran low on NS

Homework Log - *continued*

Section Name	Planned Time Strategy	Section Strategies	# Correct / Score	Notes

Practice Test Goals

Use this page to set goals before you take each practice test. Remember that goals can be about the process (things you plan to do on the test) rather than just numerical results!

After the practice test, record how you felt you did with each goal in the shaded row.

Practice Test Date	Goals for English	Goals for Math	Goals for Reading	Goals for Science
Example: 9/25	*Look for the simplest answer on mechanics questions. Remember to read the sentence before on transition questions.*			
	I remembered to find the simplest. I think I forgot to read the previous sentence on one transition question.			

Practice Test Goals - *continued*

Practice Test Date	Goals for English	Goals for Math	Goals for Reading	Goals for Science

Real Test Game Plan (Test 1)

Use this page to record your plan for your real test day. Make sure to record your observations, so you can make any necessary changes next time!

Real Test #1
Test Date:_____   Test Center:_____

Goals for English	Goals for Math	Goals for Reading	Goals for Science
Observations:			

Supplies I Need:

Snack: _____		Hair ties	
Pencils		Layers	
Eraser		Chapstick	
Calculator		Extra batteries/make sure it's charged	
Water		Admission Ticket	
ID		Outfit: _____	
Menstrual Products/Period Supplies		Other _____	

What useful, positive thoughts will help you feel confident and able?

_____

_____

_____

_____

_____

Real Test Game Place (Test 1) - *continued*

What pre-test rituals will help you feel prepared, energetic, and at your best?
The night before the test, I will _____.
For dinner, I will eat _____.
I will sleep for _____ hours.
The morning of the test, I will wake up at _____ AM.
For breakfast, I will eat _____.
To warm up my brain for the test, I will _____.
To make sure I'm feeling awake, positive, and pumped, I will _____.
Anything else: _____.

Real Test Game Plan (Test 2)

Real Test #2
Test Date:_____   Test Center:_____

Goals for English	Goals for Math	Goals for Reading	Goals for Science
Observations:			

Supplies I Need:

Snack: _____		Hair ties	
Pencils		Layers	
Eraser		Chapstick	
Calculator		Extra batteries/make sure it's charged	
Water		Admission Ticket	
ID		Outfit: _____	
Menstrual Products/Period Supplies		Other _____	

Real Test Game Plan (Test 2) - *continued*

What useful, positive thoughts will help you feel confident and able?

_____

_____

_____

_____

_____

What pre-test rituals will help you feel prepared, energetic, and at your best?
The night before the test, I will _____.
For dinner, I will eat _____.
I will sleep for _____ hours.
The morning of the test, I will wake up at _____ AM.
For breakfast, I will eat _____.
To warm up my brain for the test, I will _____.
To make sure I'm feeling awake, positive, and pumped, I will _____.
Anything else: _____.

Real Test Game Plan (Test 3)

Real Test #2
Test Date:_____   Test Center:_____

Goals for English	Goals for Math	Goals for Reading	Goals for Science
Observations:			

Supplies I Need:

Real Test Game Plan (Test 3) - *continued*

Snack: _____	Hair ties
Pencils	Layers
Eraser	Chapstick
Calculator	Extra batteries/make sure it's charged
Water	Admission Ticket
ID	Outfit: _____
Menstrual Products/Period Supplies	Other _____

What useful, positive thoughts will help you feel confident and able?

_____

_____

_____

_____

_____

What pre-test rituals will help you feel prepared, energetic, and at your best?
The night before the test, I will _____.
For dinner, I will eat _____.
I will sleep for _____ hours.
The morning of the test, I will wake up at _____ AM.
For breakfast, I will eat _____.
To warm up my brain for the test, I will _____.
To make sure I'm feeling awake, positive, and pumped, I will _____.
Anything else: _____.

Build Your Own

In this section, you have the opportunity to synthesize what you've learned about the ACT sections and challenge yourself. Follow the directions for each section to write questions and answer choices, matching the format of the ACT as closely as you can. If you can write ACT questions, you have a solid understanding of the test!

English

Directions: The first paragraphs of this passage are written for you. Fill in the answer choices and record your answers at the bottom of the section. You can test your tutor to see if they get the correct answers! Note that the NO CHANGE option for questions 1-4 may not be correct; in other words, you may have to come up with a correct alternative on your own. Then, write 1–2 paragraphs and include questions to match. Make sure to include a variety of question types. If your tutor has their own directions for the quantity and types of questions they'd like you to include, list them here:

Question Type	Number of Questions
Ex: Subject-Verb Agreement with Prepositional Phrase Break	*3*

As a dog owner, you may at times catch yourself commenting on your loyal companion's morning stretch or telling your furry friend that it's time for a well-deserved treat. You may even find yourself having a one-sided conversation about the weather or the world.
————————————————————————
  1

1. Which choice gives the most specific example of a person's interactions with their pet?

    A. NO CHANGE
    B. _____
    C. _____
    D. _____

English - *continued*

But do you ever stop to wonder if your pet can understand what you say? Scientists <u>have wondered, and have</u> created
₂
studies on this exact topic.

     Studying dogs' brains, <u>accordingly,</u> is not easy. Brain
₃
studies often use an fMRI machine, which measures blood flow in the brain to see which are being used. The dogs in this particular study needed to be trained <u>laying</u> perfectly still in a
₄

loud, unfamiliar machine. <u>Miraculously,</u> enough test subjects
₅
were studied to determine a link between words familiar and unfamiliar to dogs and the parts of their brains activated.

2.   **F.** NO CHANGE
     G. _____
     H. _____
     J. _____

3.   **A.** NO CHANGE
     B. _____
     C. _____
     D. _____

4.   **F.** NO CHANGE
     G. _____
     H. _____
     J. _____

5.   **A.** NO CHANGE
     B. _____
     C. _____
     D. _____

6.   **F.** NO CHANGE
     G. _____
     H. _____
     J. _____

7.   **A.** NO CHANGE
     B. _____
     C. _____
     D. _____

8. _____
     _____
     _____

     F. NO CHANGE
     G. _____
     H. _____
     J. _____

9.   **A.** NO CHANGE
     B. _____
     C. _____
     D. _____

10. **F.** NO CHANGE
     G. _____
     H. _____
     J. _____

Correct Answers: 1._____ 2._____ 3._____ 4._____ 5._____ 6._____ 7._____ 8._____ 9._____ 10._____

Math - *Answer Choice Formats*

Directions: Use the given answer choices to write an appropriate question to match. Make sure that your question has given information and a goal. Record your answers at the bottom of the section. You can test your tutor to see if they get the correct answers!

1. (Numbers)_____

A. -15

B. -3

C. 0

D. 4

E. 18

2. (Special Values)_____

F. $\sqrt{2}$

G. $\sqrt{3}$

H. $2\sqrt{2}$

J. $2\sqrt{3}$

K. $3\sqrt{2}$

3. (Expressions)_____

A. x^2

B. x^2y

C. $2xy^2$

D. $2x^2y$

E. $4x^2y^2$

4. (Phrases)_____

F. A circle

G. An Ellipse

H. A parabola

J. A hyperbola

K. Cannot be determined from the given information

5. (Visuals)_____

A. 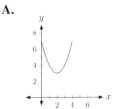 D.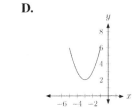

B. 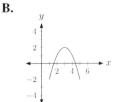 E.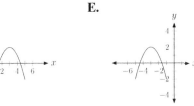

C.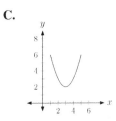

Correct Answers: 1._____ 2._____ 3._____ 4._____ 5._____

Math - *Question Types*

Directions: Write the answer choices to go along with each question type. Fill in the answer choices and record your answers at the bottom of the section. You can test your tutor to see if they get the correct answers!

1. A daycare charges $30 to join and then $10 for each hour a child stays. Which of the following equations models the relationship between c, the total cost of daycare, and h, the number of hours a student attends?

    A.

    B.

    C.

    D.

    E.

2. Which of the following is equivalent to $a^3b^5c^4(a^4b^7c^2)^{1/2}$

    F.

    G.

    H.

    J.

    K.

3. Which of the following inequalities describes the solution set for $4x + 7 \geq -2x - 12?$

    A.

    B.

    C.

    D.

    E.

4. A 10-foot flagpole casts a shadow that is 14 feet long. Which of the following expresses the angle of elevation from the end of the shadow to the top of the flagpole? (Note: Express your answer in terms of sin^{-1}, cos^{-1}, or tan^{-1})

    F.

    G.

    H.

    J.

    K.

5. A circle is inscribed in a square. The area of the square is 256 cm^2. In terms of pi, which of the following is the circumference of the circle?

    A.

    B.

    C.

    D.

    E.

Correct Answers: 1._____ 2._____ 3._____ 4._____ 5._____

Math - *Question Types*

Directions: Write a question for each question type. Include 5 answer choices for each, and use nonnumerical answers for at least half of the problems. Fill in the answer choices and record your answers at the bottom of the section. You can test your tutor to see if they get the answers correct!

Cluster Question

Initial Information(with space for visual):

1. Word Problem:_____
   _____
   _____
   _____

   A.

   B.

   C.

   D.

   E.

2. Expression Based:_____
   _____
   _____
   _____

   F.

   G.

   H.

   J.

   K.

3. Visual Based:_____
   _____
   _____

   Visual:

   A.

   B.

   C.

   D.

   E.

4. _____
   _____
   _____
   _____

   F.
   G.
   H.
   J.
   K.

5. _____
   _____
   _____
   _____

   A.
   B.
   C.
   D.
   E.

6. _____
   _____
   _____
   _____

   F.
   G.
   H.
   J.
   K.

Correct Answers: 1._____ 2._____ 3._____ 4._____ 5._____ 6._____

Directions: Read and annotate the passage below. Then, use the passage to complete the questions and answer choices.

LITERARY NARRATIVE: This passage is adapted from *The Great Gatsby* by F. Scott Fitzgerald.

About halfway between West Egg and New York the motor road hastily joins the railroad and runs beside it for a quarter of a mile, so as to shrink away from a certain des-olate area of land. This is a valley of ashes—a fantastic
5 farm where ashes grow like wheat into ridges and hills and grotesque gardens; where ashes take the forms of houses and chimneys and rising smoke and, finally, with a transcen-dent effort, of ash-grey men, who move dimly and already crumbling through the powdery air. Occasionally a line of
10 grey cars crawls along an invisible track, gives out a ghastly creak, and comes to rest, and immediately the ash-grey men swarm up with leaden spades and stir up an impenetrable cloud, which screens their obscure operations from your sight.

15 But above the grey land and the spasms of bleak dust which drift endlessly over it, you perceive, after a moment, the eyes of Doctor T. J. Eckleburg. The eyes of Doctor T. J. Eckleburg are blue and gigantic—their retinas are one yard high. They look out of no face, but, instead, from a pair of
20 enormous yellow spectacles which pass over a nonexistent nose. Evidently some wild wag of an oculist set them there to fatten his practice in the borough of Queens, and then sank down himself into eternal blindness, or forgot them and moved away. But his eyes, dimmed a little by many
25 paintless days, under sun and rain, brood on over the solemn dumping ground.

The valley of ashes is bounded on one side by a small foul river, and, when the drawbridge is up to let barges through, the passengers on waiting trains can stare at the
30 dismal scene for as long as half an hour. There is always a halt there of at least a minute, and it was because of this that I first met Tom Buchanan's mistress.

The fact that he had one was insisted upon wherever he was known. His acquaintances resented the fact that he
35 turned up in popular cafés with her and, leaving her at a table, sauntered about, chatting with whomsoever he knew. Though I was curious to see her, I had no desire to meet her—but I did. I went up to New York with Tom on the train one afternoon, and when we stopped by the ash-heaps
40 he jumped to his feet and,taking hold of my elbow, literally forced me from the car.

"We're getting off," he insisted. "I want you to meet my girl."

I think he'd tanked up a good deal at luncheon, and his
45 determination to have my company bordered on violence. The supercilious assumption was that on Sunday afternoon I had nothing better to do.

I followed him over a low whitewashed railroad fence, and we walked back a hundred yards along the road under
50 Doctor Eckleburg's persistent stare. The only building in sight was a small block of yellow brick sitting on the edge of the waste land, a sort of compact Main Street minister-ing to it, and contiguous to absolutely nothing. One of the three shops it contained was for rent and another was an
55 all-night restaurant, approached by a trail of ashes; the third was a garage—Repairs. George B. Wilson. Cars bought and sold.—and I followed Tom inside.

The interior was unprosperous and bare; the only car vis-ible was the dust-covered wreck of a Ford which crouched
60 in a dim corner. It had occurred to me that this shadow of a garage must be a blind, and that sumptuous and romantic apartments were concealed overhead, when the proprietor himself appeared in the door of an office, wiping his hands on a piece of waste. He was a blond, spiritless man, anaemic,
65 and faintly handsome. When he saw us a damp gleam of hope sprang into his light blue eyes.

"Hello, Wilson, old man," said Tom, slapping him jovially on the shoulder. "How's business?"

"I can't complain," answered Wilson unconvincingly.
70 "When are you going to sell me that car?"

"Next week; I've got my man working on it now."

"Works pretty slow, don't he?"

"No, he doesn't," said Tom coldly. "And if you feel that way about it, maybe I'd better sell it somewhere else after
75 all."

"I don't mean that," explained Wilson quickly. "I just meant—"

His voice faded off and Tom glanced impatiently around the garage.

Reading - *The Questions*

Directions: In numbers 1-3, write the answer choices to match the given question. In numbers 4-6, write the question to match the given answer choices. In numbers 7-10, write a question and answer choices to match the question type. Fill in the answer choices and record your answers at the bottom of the section. You can test your tutor to see if they get the correct answers!

1. The main purpose of the fourth paragraph (lines 33-34) is to:

   A. _____
   B. _____
   C. _____
   D. _____

2. The main idea of the passage is that:

   F. _____
   G. _____
   H. _____
   J. _____

3. Which of the following does NOT accurately match the passage's description of the garage?

   A. _____
   B. _____
   C. _____
   D. _____

4. _____
   _____
   _____

   F. ecstatic.
   G. confused.
   H. disgusted.
   J. irate

5. _____
   _____
   _____

   A. explain why people should never drive along the motor road.
   B. illustrate the difficult circumstances of railroad workers.
   C. prove Doctor Eckleburg's reasoning for a billboard location.
   D. provide a description of a barren landscape.

6. _____
   _____
   _____

   F. visit Tom's mistress.
   G. have lunch in a popular café.
   H. get their car fixed at a garage.
   J. visit a relative of Tom.

7. Tier 1, Purpose_____
   _____

   A. _____
   B. _____
   C. _____
   D. _____

8. Tier 2, Specific Detail_____
   _____

   F. _____
   G. _____
   H. _____
   J. _____

9. Tier 2, Main Idea_____
   _____

   A. _____
   B. _____
   C. _____
   D. _____

10. Tier 3, Specific detail_____
    _____

    F. _____
    G. _____
    H. _____
    J. _____

Correct Answers: 1._____ 2._____ 3._____ 4._____ 5._____ 6._____ 7._____ 8._____ 9._____ 10._____

Science - *Passage*

Directions: Use the passage that follows to write questions and answers to match. Each question specifies the question type you should write. Fill in the answer choices and record your answers at the bottom of the section. You can test your tutor to see if they get the correct answers! Remember that questions should increase in difficulty.

Experiment 1

Six French marigolds (*Tagetes patula*) seeds were planted in separate 900 cm^3 soiled pots. Each pot received a different amount of water per day, for 10 days. The plant height, in centimeters, at the end of the 10th day was recorded as shown in Table 1.

Experiment 2

Five *T. patula* seeds were planted in separate 900 cm^3 soiled pots containing different quantities of phosphorus. Each plant was watered with 15mL of water per day, for 10 days. Table 2 shows the amount of phosphorus, in ppm, of each soil type. Figure 1 shows the plant height, in centimeters, for each soil type at the end of the 10th day

Table 1		
Pot	Amount of Water per day (mL)	Plant Height (cm)
1	0	0
2	5	2.1
3	10	3.5
4	15	4.4
5	20	2.7
6	25	0.4

Table 2		
Pot	Soil Type (mL)	Amount of Phosphorus (ppm)
7	A	0
8	B	20
9	C	40
10	D	60
11	E	80

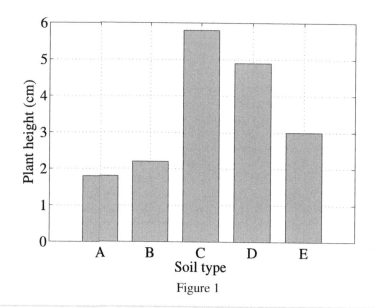

Figure 1

Science - *Questions*

1. Question Type: Locating_____
_____
_____

   A. _____
   B. _____
   C. _____
   D. _____

2. Question Type: Trends_____
_____
_____

   F. _____
   G. _____
   H. _____
   J. _____

3. Question Type: Data Bridge_____
_____
_____

   A. _____
   B. _____
   C. _____
   D. _____

4. Question Type: Independent/Dependent Variable _____
_____
_____

   F. _____
   G. _____
   H. _____
   J. _____

5. Question Type: Last Question _____
_____

   A. _____
   B. _____
   C. _____
   D. _____

Correct Answers: 1.____ 2.____ 3.____ 4.____ 5.____

ABOUT PRIVATE PREP

Private Prep is an education services company that offers individually customized lessons in all K-12 academic subjects, standardized test prep, and college admissions consulting. We believe personal attention is fundamental to academic achievement and lies at the forefront of every student-tutor relationship. Designing curriculum for each student's unique learning style, we focus not only on improving grades and increasing test scores but also on building confidence and developing valuable skills—like work ethic, growth mindset, and anxiety management—that will last a lifetime.

One of the most significant points of differentiation between us and other educational services companies is our team approach. Our directors work in tandem with tutors and support staff to provide comprehensive, collaborative support to families.

We also focus on giving back to the communities in which we work. Through the Private Prep Scholarship Program, we place high-achieving students from low-income or underserved backgrounds with individual tutors, who work with them to navigate the test prep and college application process and ultimately gain admission to best-fit colleges.

At Private Prep, we deliver a superior academic experience—in the U.S., abroad, and online—that is supported by diverse and excellent resources in recruitment, curriculum design, professional training, and custom software development.

Made in the USA
Middletown, DE
17 June 2021